CW01651094

DUBLIN ZOO

Elephants

Written by Catherine de Courcy | Illustrated by Cathy Callan
Art Direction by Anne Brady

Meet the Elephants

Dublin Zoo's elephants are all Asian elephants. Their bodies are different sizes and shapes but it can be difficult to identify them by name when they are standing apart. One way of getting to know each elephant is by noticing the way their ears fold.

Yasmin: Born 25 November 1990, Rotterdam Zoo. Sister of Bernhardine.

Bernhardine: Born 16 June 1984, Rotterdam Zoo. Oldest female in the herd, which means she is in charge. She has no hair on her tail and has a bony back.

Upali: Born 14 November 1994, Zurich Zoo. Only male elephant in the Dublin Zoo herd. He is the biggest elephant in the herd and has tusks.

Anak: Born 26 July 2003, Rotterdam Zoo. Daughter of Yasmin. Anak has little tusks – known as *tushes*.

Asha: Born 7 May 2007. Daughter of Bernhardine and the first elephant to be born in Dublin Zoo.

Elephants at The Kaziranga Forest Trail, Dublin Zoo

Elephants are social and intelligent animals. In the wild, they live in family groups. Older elephants pass on information and skills to the younger generation. The eldest female is usually in charge and is known as the matriarch.

In this picture, Bernhardine is watching her daughter, Asha, and her niece, Anak, play by the water.

Young male elephants leave the family group when they are old enough to join a young all-male group. When they mature into adulthood, they live alone but visit the females to mate.

Upali, the bull elephant, has his own space but he chooses to spend much of his time with the females. Here, he is expressing interest in Yasmin on the right.

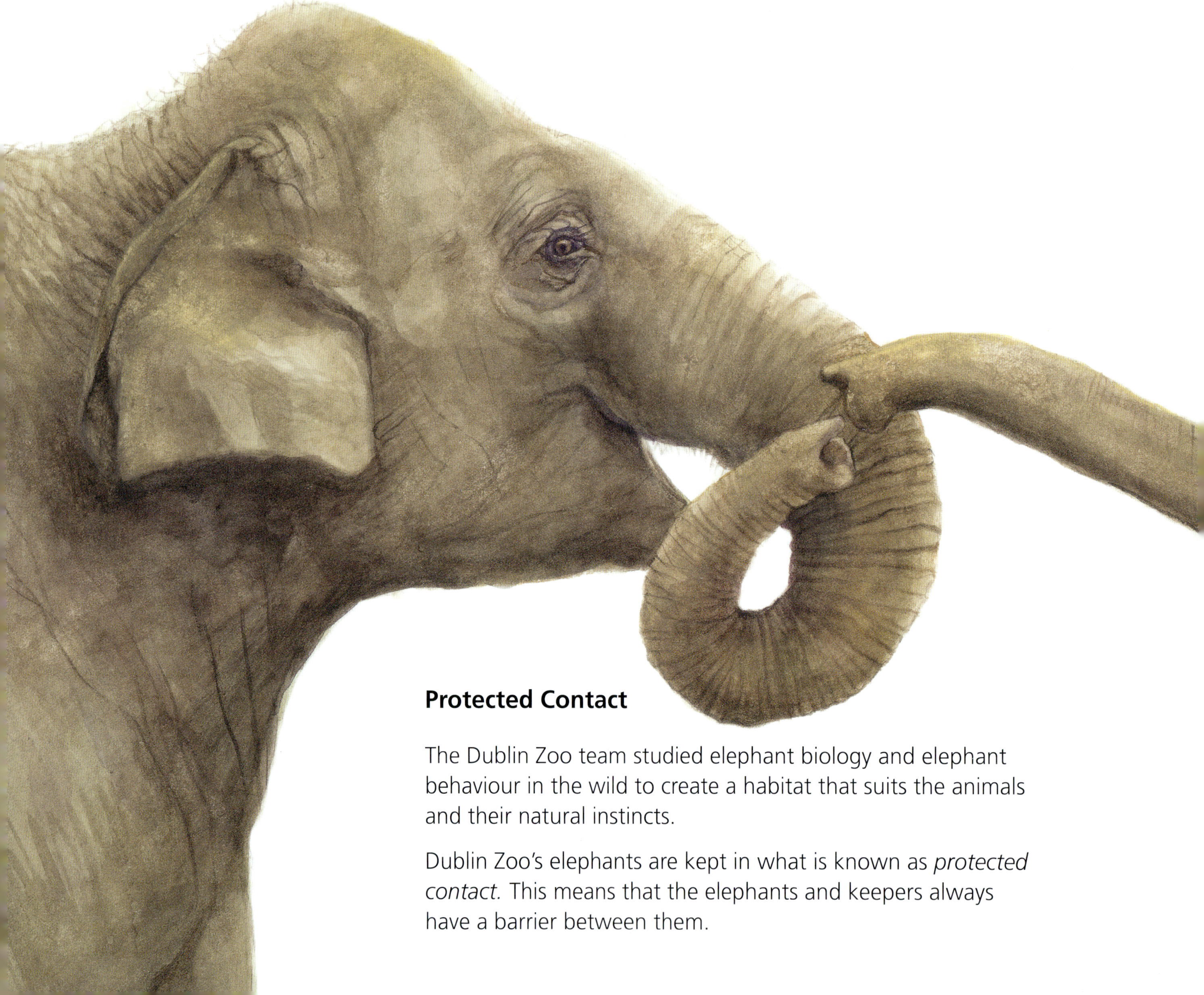

Protected Contact

The Dublin Zoo team studied elephant biology and elephant behaviour in the wild to create a habitat that suits the animals and their natural instincts.

Dublin Zoo's elephants are kept in what is known as *protected contact.* This means that the elephants and keepers always have a barrier between them.

This allows the elephants to live in a natural family group without humans telling them what to do. When the keepers want to carry out health checks, they call the elephants to the barrier. If an elephant does not want to go to the keepers, it will just ignore them or walk away.

Early Morning in the Female Elephants' House

All of the female elephants sleep in one house. They sleep for four or five hours each night. They never lie down for longer than an hour at a time because they are very heavy animals and they need to change position to shift their weight. They dig their feet into the sand to help themselves stand up.

Each evening, the keepers leave plenty of food in the elephant house; they also leave the doors into the outdoor habitat open. This means that the elephants can feed and go outside during the night if they wish.

The roof of the house is made of glass so the elephants know when it is morning.

On one occasion, all of the females went out into a rainstorm. As the lightning flashed, they trumpeted and flapped their ears; then they went for a swim.

Elephant Husbandry

In the wild, elephants walk over rough ground for many kilometres. They swim. They rub against rough surfaces. This keeps their muscles strong, their skin clean and their feet in good condition.

The power washer is used by the keeper to clean dirt from their feet and legs.

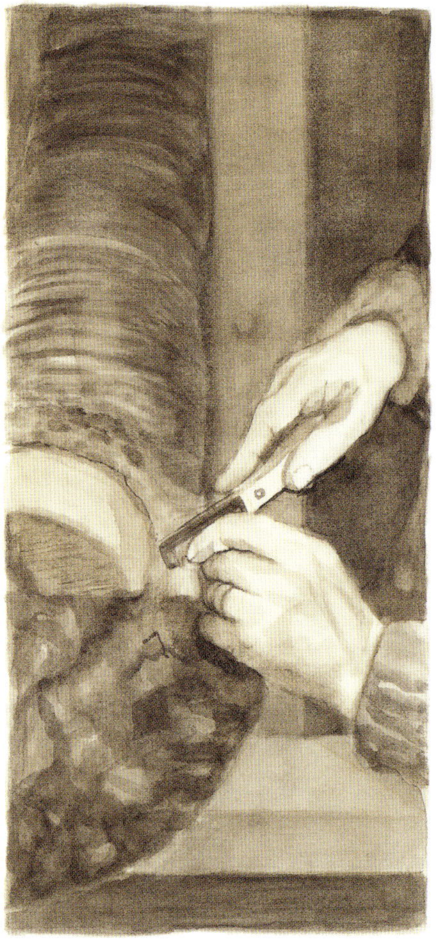

Foot and nail hygiene is very important because if their feet are not kept very clean, they can become infected. The sand used at The Kaziranga Forest Trail is coarse estuary sand that helps to clean their feet naturally.

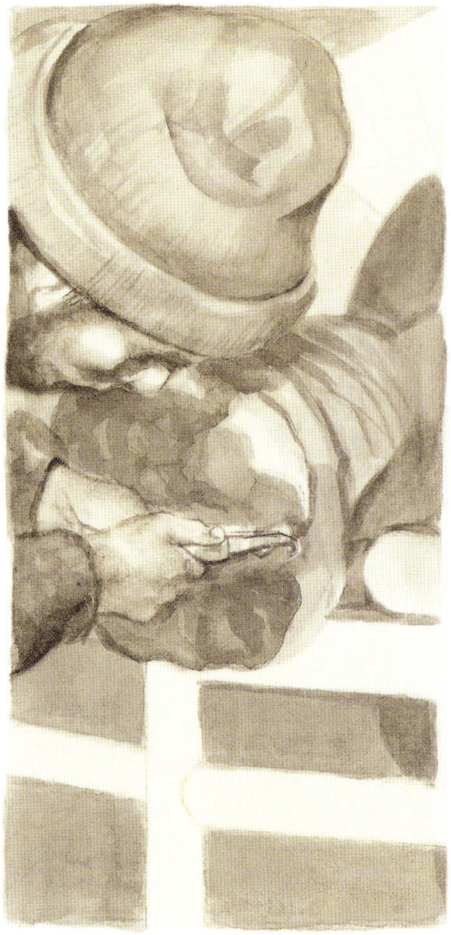

At least once a week, the keepers examine the elephants' nails and feet. They also file the elephants' nails when necessary.

In Dublin Zoo, rough sand, pools and rocky surfaces help the elephants to care for themselves. But the keepers also need to do some additional work to make sure that the elephants all remain healthy.

This work, carried out in the mornings, is known as *husbandry* and it is done through the barriers with the elephants' cooperation.

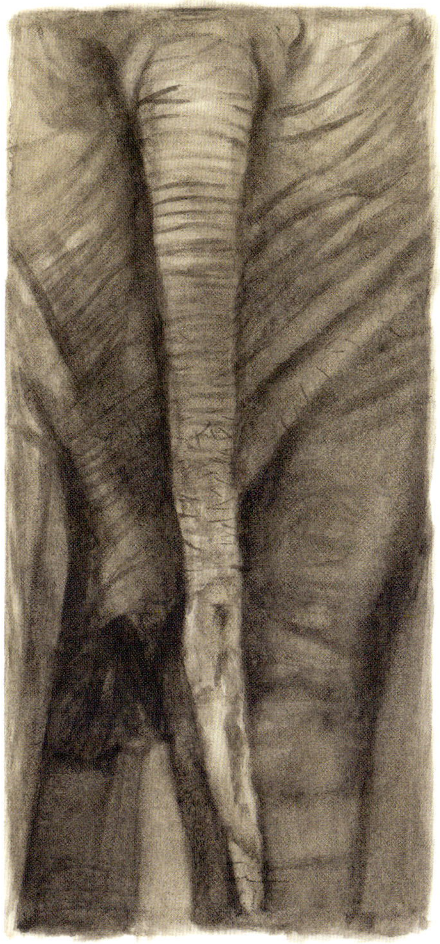

Moisturising the tail keeps the skin supple.

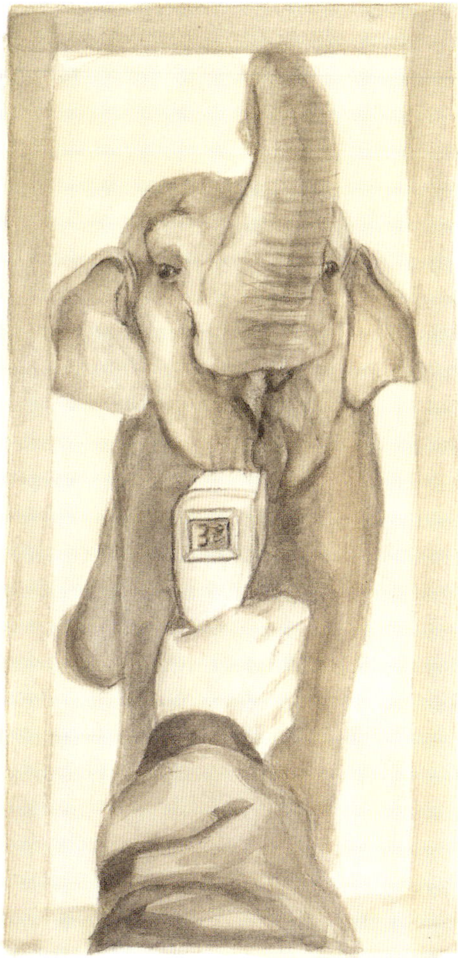

This picture shows a keeper taking the elephant's temperature with a hand-held thermometer. A small change in temperature could indicate that there is a medical problem.

The elephants walk across a weighbridge on the way to their habitat each morning and keepers record their weight. A big change in weight could indicate that there is a medical problem.

Early Morning in the Bull House

The mature male Upali has his own house with an outdoor space. Upali is very strong; his house is heavily reinforced because he likes to test his strength against the walls.

Upali also gets a shower and health check every morning. He likes the keepers to work on his feet and he is very cooperative. But if he is disturbed by a loud noise or a bird, he will walk away from the keepers, even if they have not finished working on his feet.

As soon as the elephants go to their outdoor space, the keepers clean the sand in their houses. Dung is removed. The sand is turned and water is sprinkled on it so that the urine washes through it. They put in plenty of food for the elephants for the following evening.

The Daily Greeting

When Upali and the female elephants leave their houses, they greet each other in the habitat. If the females are very excited, they may rush to meet Upali, flapping their ears and trumpeting. When they are calm, they will sniff and rub against each other.

Gerry: 'Bernhardine, or Dina as we call her, is the matriarch at The Kaziranga Forest Trail. She came from Rotterdam Zoo and has adapted to life in Dublin Zoo to become a great leader. She is cool, calm and deliberate and eager to please. Her influence on the herd is very strong; her approach is to show strength with compassion.'

Eating All Day

In the wild, elephants eat for about sixteen hours each day. They eat grasses, leaves, tree branches and some fruit. They dig up salt and other minerals from wet ground. They do not eat meat.

In Dublin Zoo, food is provided for elephants throughout the day and night. Hay is central to their diet and together they eat twelve bales every day. The hay is put into baskets high above their heads. Only the bigger elephants can reach it. The smaller elephants eat what falls to the ground. They have to work hard with their trunks gathering neat bundles of hay to put into their mouths.

It takes the elephants at least two hours to empty the high basket of hay. If the hay was put on the ground in front of them, they would eat it in thirty minutes. Having to reach for the hay exercises their trunks.

Foraging for Food

The keepers hide food around The Kaziranga Forest Trail so the elephants have to use their instincts and skills to find it.

The elephants often look for chopped vegetables and fruit buried in the sand.

Branches of trees, known as browse, are another favourite elephant food. Using their trunks and their legs, they slowly strip leaves, twigs and branches off the main branch. When they get to a thick piece, they will hit it against something hard to soften it.

An elephant drinks up to 250 litres of water every day; they can suck up to eight litres of water into their trunk at a time; they squirt the water from their trunks into their mouths.

Apples and other surprises are put into food balls with small openings; the elephants have to shake the food out of them.

Elephants produce dung up to twenty times a day and between them make 400 to 500 kilograms of dung each day. The dung is sent to an organic farm in Ireland to be used as fertiliser.

Family Life

Life at The Kaziranga Forest Trail is harmonious. The elephants like to walk, play, swim and communicate with each other. They are very affectionate and will use their ears, tails and their trunks to indicate pleasure in each other's company.

Sometimes Yasmin wants to take on the role of matriarch and squabbles with Bernhardine. On occasion Asha and Anak may become too boisterous when they are playing. But the elephants sort out their problems amongst themselves.

Brendan: 'Blackbuck are an Indian antelope that share the same habitat as the Asian elephants in the wild. In Dublin Zoo, blackbuck live at The Kaziranga Forest Trail. They are not afraid of the elephants and they have plenty of places to run away to where the elephants can't follow.'

Upali is very gentle with the young elephants and allows them to play with him. If he gets tired of them, he swishes his tail, pushes them away and returns to his own house.

Alice: 'Dublin Zoo elephants have a unique sound which they use to communicate with each other. Meike Artelt, a scientist who records elephant sounds, said that she has never heard the Dublin elephant sound anywhere else. She believes it is specific to our elephants. It is a bit like the call of a bird. It can be loud or low or in different tones. The young elephants use it if they are anxious and then the mothers come running to them.'

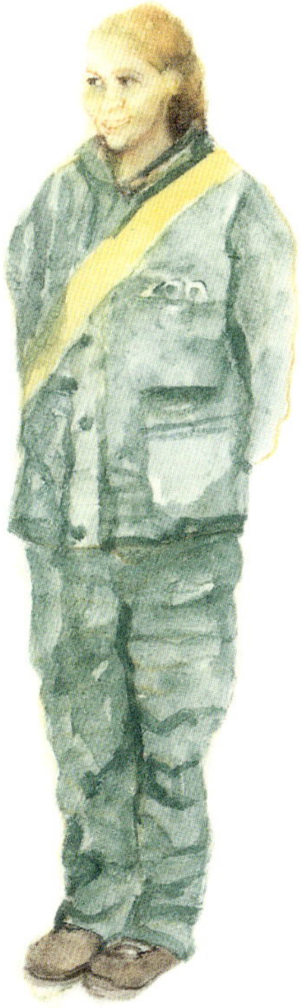

The Elephant's Trunk

Yasmin sucking up water into her mouth.

Anak touching Upali in an affectionate way.

Bernhardine, the matriarch, sniffs the air for rain.

The elephant's trunk is made up mostly of muscle. It has no bones and is very flexible. Elephants use it to do many things and their trunks are often in motion.

They breathe through their trunks and have a very acute sense of smell.

The tips of their trunks are sensitive and can be used like fingers. Mothers teach their young how to use their trunks. Elephants show affection by touching each other with their trunks.

Anak putting her trunk into Yasmin's mouth as a sign of trust.

Communicating

Asha puts her trunk into her mouth to make noises such as a squeak or rumble.

Bernhardine throwing wet sand on her back as a sunscreen and to moisturise her skin. An elephant's skin is thick but sensitive to sunlight; they also blow mud and wood chips on their backs.

Swimming

Elephants are natural swimmers. There are two deep pools at The Kaziranga Forest Trail and the elephants love swimming there on a fine day. Swimming exercises their muscles and it is very good for their skin. They play in the water, pushing each other in and jumping on top of each other. They often duck under the water and breathe through their trunks.

In this picture (opposite), Upali, on the left with his back to us, is swimming with Asha and Anak while Bernhardine and Yasmin watch.

Donal: 'Anak is very intelligent and confident and very determined. Anak was in the pool the first time Asha got into the water. The pool is very deep and Asha was very young and quickly got into difficulty. Asha called out in distress. Anak swam around, hooked Asha with her trunk, scooped her out and ushered her to the steps. Anak would not let Asha into the pool for a few weeks after that. Asha is now a very confident swimmer.'

Elephant Calves in Dublin Zoo

When Bernhardine and Yasmin arrived in Dublin in 2006 from Rotterdam Zoo, they were both pregnant. Anak, Yasmin's daughter, then aged three, came with them.

An elephant pregnancy lasts for twenty-two months. Asha was born in Dublin Zoo in 2007.

Budi, a male elephant, was born in 2008.

In this scene from 2008, Budi is mimicking the way his mother is lifting her feet.

Birth of Asha

Asha was born during the night. In the wild, elephant calves are usually born when it is still dark. A newborn elephant might be attacked by a predator if it cannot walk with the herd by daybreak.

Asha was born on deep sand. With Yasmin's help, Bernhardine cleaned Asha and nudged her with her trunk to help her stand. Within ten minutes of her birth, Asha took her first steps. Anak watched the older females closely.

Asha could reach her mother's breast to suckle when she stood up. She weighed eighty kilograms when she was born; this weight is similar to that of an adult human.

The keepers watched through a camera in the director's office. They were anxious in case anything went wrong but they let the elephants manage the birth by themselves without interfering.

Asha as a Calf

Asha learns skills from her mother, Bernhardine, and her aunt, Yasmin. Anak (on the left) watches the older elephants with the young calf and learns mothering techniques from them.

Louise: 'Asha is sweet, gentle and mischievous. She is also a peacemaker. When Bernhardine and Yasmin squabble, Asha will put her trunk in their mouths to calm them down. Asha is the matriarch's daughter and that gives her an important role in the herd'.

'Asha has never seen a human in her space. She is one of the oldest elephants in any zoo who has known only protected contact.'

Budi, the Male Elephant Born in Dublin Zoo

Yasmin gave birth to Budi in February 2008. Bernhardine helped with the birth. Anak was also able to help because she had watched Asha's birth.

Budi was very boisterous as a young calf. He loved playing with Asha and Anak. As he grew older and stronger, Bernhardine and Yasmin had to control his lively behaviour.

In the wild, young bull elephants are pushed out of the herd by the older females as they mature. They join an all-male group where they can test their strength against other young bulls and learn the behaviours they will need when they are adults.

In July 2012 Budi went to Belgium to join an all-male group in Antwerp Zoo, where they also use protected contact.

James: 'Yasmin, Budi's mother, is a complicated elephant who can go off into a day-dream. But she is a very good and nurturing mother. Even when Budi's tusks were sharp and dug into her, she still allowed him to suckle her. She didn't mind Budi wandering around the habitat without her because he was so confident. But if Budi called out in distress, Yasmin would run to him.'

Upali, the Dublin Zoo Bull Elephant

In July 2012, the arrival of Upali changed many things at The Kaziranga Forest Trail. Now the females could interact with an adult male elephant, mate, become pregnant and hopefully give birth to healthy calves, which they would then raise.

Before Upali arrived, the keepers put some of his dung into the females' habitat. Elephants learn a lot about each other from the smell of each other's urine or dung; the females were able to prepare for Upali's arrival by getting used to his scent. By the time of their first meeting, the female elephants were so excited that they trumpeted, roared, squealed, flapped their ears, swished their tails and blew air at him.

Now Dublin Zoo has a small but complete herd of elephants.

Ciaran: 'Upali is very calm animal and is used to adult females and calves. He is very intelligent and masterful. He walks around the habitat calmly and slowly. Lots of bulls won't tolerate calves but Upali is very gentle with them. Upali has warning signals if he wants to be away from the females. He likes his own time to himself.'

'When Upali first met the females, Bernhardine, who had lived with an adult bull in Rotterdam Zoo, knew exactly what to do. She turned her back on him, raised her tail and urinated. Upali smelt her. The other females, watching the matriarch, followed her example. This natural behaviour calmed them all.'

Mating

Upali and the female elephants accepted each other very quickly. After some time taking with each other's scent, they were ready to mate. Upali went into the condition known as *musth*. The females followed him around, smelt him and then allowed him to mate with them. Mating is very quick.

Bernhardine was the first to become pregnant, then Yasmin, Anak and finally Asha. The new baby elephants are expected in 2014 and 2015. They will be born into a circle where their mother, aunt, sister and cousin will all help with the births. They will be raised under the loving guidance of the matriarch and the extended family group, including Upali because he is very good with calves.

Sophie: 'We put different coloured glitter into a banana for each elephant. The glitter is harmless and is not digested so that it appears in the dung. This allows the keepers to identify whose dung is whose. When we analyse the dung, we get information about the general health of the elephants; we can also find out when one of the females is pregnant. This is Bernhardine's dung because the glitter is red. She was the first of our elephants to become pregnant by Upali.'

Going to bed, in the same house!

The affectionate relationship between all of the elephants at The Kaziranga Forest Trail has created an unusual situation. Normally in zoos, the female elephants return to their house at the end of the day while the bull returns to his because adult male elephants normally sleep alone in the wild. But, in Dublin Zoo, the females have followed Upali into his house on many occasions and Upali has allowed them to stay with him for the night.

Ciaran: 'In the wild, the bull elephant would stay with the females when they are willing to mate. So when Upali wants the females around during the night, we don't interfere. We leave plenty of food so there is no squabbling. We also keep an eye on them on the remote cameras. It is magic to see them all together'.

Reference

AFRICAN ELEPHANTS AND ASIAN ELEPHANTS: MAJOR DIFFERENCES
The species of elephant in Dublin Zoo is the Asian elephant. Another species of elephant does exist, the African elephant. It is possible to tell the difference between African and Asian elephants by a few key features. (See diagram on opposite page).

Elephants in the wild can live to about sixty years old.

LEGS AND FEET
When elephants walk, they usually lift two feet on one side while their other feet remain on the ground. They walk, run and swim but do not trot, gallop or jump. They can move quickly and outrun most humans. Elephants sway to help the circulation of blood from their feet back to their heart.

Asian elephants usually have five toenails on their front feet and four on their back. Each toenail has a cuticle, like a human nail. The soles of the elephant's feet are made up of pads of soft tissue. This allows elephants to walk quietly in a forest and gives them sure footing on uneven or swampy ground.

Photo: Maxi (right), Upali's father, in Zurich Zoo. With big tusks, he is known as a 'tusker'.

SKELETON, SKULL AND TUSKS
Elephants have over 200 bones and nineteen or twenty ribs and the ribcage extends along the backbone

The bone of an elephant's skull is honeycombed rather than solid; this means that it is lighter than it looks, yet it is extremely strong.

Tusks are an elephant's two front teeth, which are known as incisors. The tusks are used for stripping bark off trees, digging for food and in defense. Tusks continue to grow during an elephant's lifetime and in some elephants can grow to nearly three metres.

Elephants usually have two molars and two tusks in the upper jaw and two molars in the lower jaw. The teeth continue to grow and are replaced when worn, about six times throughout their lives.

INTERNAL ORGANS
The brain of an elephant is larger than any other land mammal and is located at the back of its skull.

The weight of an elephant's heart is between twelve and twenty-one kilograms. A standing, resting elephant's heart beats between thirty and forty times a minute. Its heart rate increases when it lies down.

An elephant's stomach is used largely for storing food; digestion takes place in the large intestine. The combined length of an elephant's small and large intestines can reach thirty-five metres!

An elephant's trunk is its nose and upper lip fused together. Elephants breathe through their trunk about seventy percent of the time. Elephants also use their trunks as snorkels when swimming underwater.

DAILY DIET IN DUBLIN ZOO
The fibre diet of Dublin Zoo's elephants is very close to the fibre diet of elephants in the wild. This is daily menu for all five elephants in Dublin Zoo:

20 tree branches, known as browse
12 bales of hay
15 kg of pellets, with calcium and vitamin E for the females.
10kg of fruit
8 kg of carrots
8 kg of turnips
Nuts

Each elephant drinks up to 250 litres of water a day.

ELEPHANT COMMUNICATION
Elephants communicate with body language and sound. Their sounds include rumbles, growls, roars, screams and squeals, and trumpeting. They also make very low sounds that humans cannot hear. This type of communication is called infrasound. In the wild they use infrasound to communicate with other elephants over long distances about availability of food and water or about threats and dangers.

EARS
Elephants use their ears to keep cool. By flapping their ears, they cool down the blood in the vessels of their ears. As the cooler blood flows though their bulky bodies, it helps them to regulate their temperature.

ELEPHANT SKIN
The skin of an elephant is very thick around its back and sides and has ridges and creases throughout. It is hairy when an elephant is very young but loses hair as it gets older. In the wild elephants keep their skin supple and free of parasites by wallowing in mud, scratching against trees, submerging in water, and covering themselves with dust. Mud and dust work as a sunscreen on hot days.

In Dublin Zoo, the elephants get a daily shower and can swim in the pools. They have sand to throw on their backs in their habitat. They also have rough walls in their houses to scratch themselves against and rocks in the habitat to give themselves a belly scratch.

African Elephant

Asian Elephant

MAJOR DIFFERENCES BETWEEN AFRICAN ELEPHANTS AND ASIAN ELEPHANTS

- The African elephant's ears are bigger than the Asian elephant's ears, and are fan-shaped.
- All African elephants have tusks. Male Asian elephants usually have tusks but female Asian elephants may only have small tusks known as *tushes*.
- African elephants are generally larger than Asian elephants.
- The African elephant has two lips or *fingers* on its trunk but the Asian elephant has only one.
- The African elephant has a single dome on its forehead and the Asian elephant has twin mounds.

Dublin Zoo and Conservation of Asian Elephants

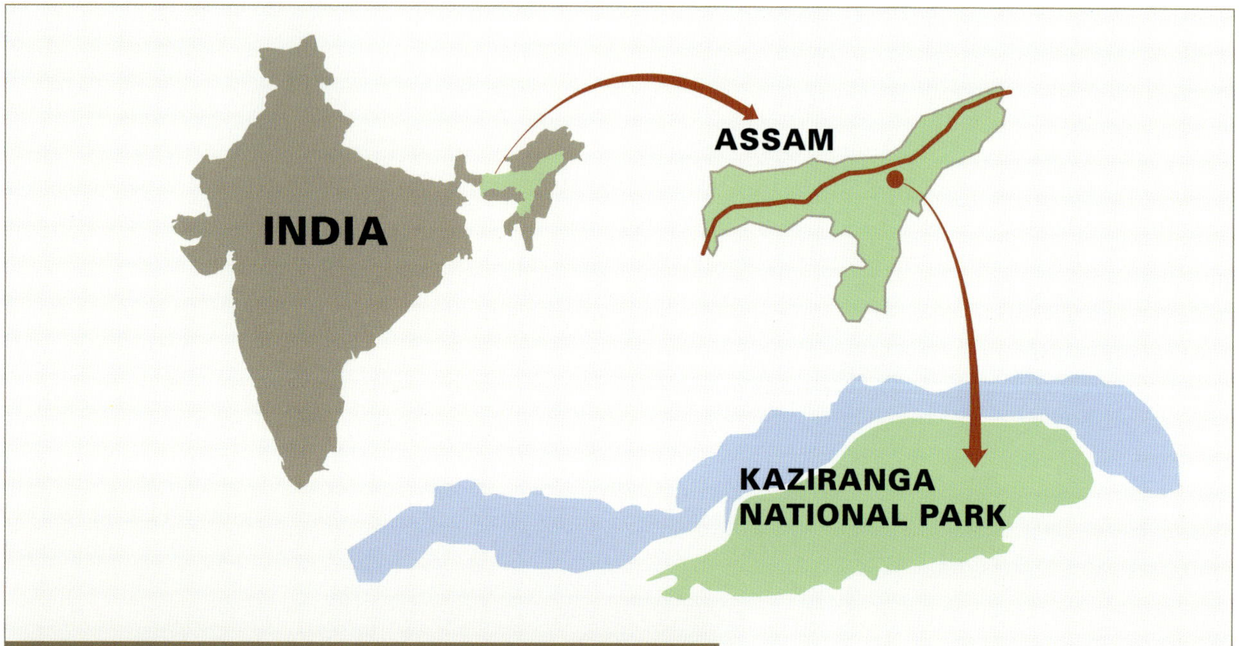

Location of Kaziranga National Park in India

REASONS WHY ASIAN ELEPHANTS ARE ENDANGERED:

- Humans want the ivory from their tusks and kill elephants for it. Elephants with large tusks are known as *tuskers*.
- Forests are cut down as the increasing human population needs farm land, firewood and building materials. Branches and leaves are an important part of the elephants' diet and, without lots of forest jungle, elephants may not get enough food to eat.
- In the past elephants walked for many hundreds of kilometres to eat branches and leaves. This allowed forests to re-grow after the elephants had eaten enough and moved on. Now elephants are confined to smaller spaces. Forests do not have time to re-grow before the elephants need to eat there again.
- As forests are cut down and the land is used for farming, the traditional routes elephants used in search of food and water are being destroyed.
- Elephants are dangerous to humans. With reduced forests and fewer traditional trails to follow, elephants can stray on to farms and so threaten the lives of farming families. They are then chased away and often killed.
- Young elephants learn skills and acquire information from their elders. If older elephants are killed or die, the young elephants have to learn by themselves.

ASIAN ELEPHANTS IN THE WILD

Asian elephants live in regions of South and South-East Asia where they have access to forest, water and grassland. It is believed that the largest population of wild Asian elephants is now in India. There are also populations of a few thousand wild elephants in each of Sri Lanka, Myanmar (Burma), Thailand, Malaysia and Indonesia.

Elephants have no natural predators. They are the largest living land mammals. Humans are their only threat.

ASIAN ELEPHANTS ARE ENDANGERED

Once, thousands of years ago, there may have been millions of elephants roaming Asia. As human populations increased and people needed more land to grow food and to live on, elephants lost the use of that land and their populations became smaller.

In the early twentieth century, it is believed that there were hundreds of thousands of wild Asian elephants.

Now, in the twenty-first century, it is estimated that there are only between 30,000 and 60,000 wild elephants.

The threats to Asian elephants are ever present, including poaching, habitat loss and political instability. Local and international efforts to protect their natural habitats continue in the hope of allowing wild elephants to live without being disturbed by humans.

CONSERVATION – WHAT DUBLIN ZOO IS DOING

Dublin Zoo keeps Asian elephants because they are endangered. Bernhardine, Yasmin, Anak, Asha, Upali and Budi are all registered in an international studbook. This makes them part of an international breeding programme. One of the reasons why Budi moved to Antwerp was to allow him to father young calves in a different part of the world when he is older. This way he may contribute to the genetic diversity in the elephant populations in zoos.

Dublin Zoo is supporting conservation programmes in the Kaziranga National Park in Assam, India (see map on opposite page). The Kaziranga National Park is 387 square kilometres and it is estimated that nearly 2000 elephants live here with other wildlife, such as Indian rhinoceros, tigers, panthers and many kinds of birds.

PROTECTED CONTACT AND THE HEALTH OF DUBLIN ZOO'S ELEPHANTS

Photo: Jimmy Kenny (below left) in the 1930s with Sarah the elephant

Dublin Zoo's elephants are now kept in *protected contact*. In the past, the elephants in Dublin Zoo were kept in *free contact*. This meant that there were times when there was no barrier between the keepers and the elephants. Up to the 1960s, visitors were allowed to feed the elephants and even to ride on them.

TRAINING

Photo: Dublin Zoo keeper (below) using a target with one of the elephants

Working with elephants through barriers is known as protected contact training. The barrier through which the keepers work is known as the training wall. All of the training is to allow the keepers to carry out essential health and hygiene checks on the elephants.

The elephants are encouraged to come to the keepers, who stand behind the barriers. The keepers have a long stick, which is known as a target. The keeper touches the elephant gently with the target and the elephant is trained to lift its leg or to turn around in response. Every time the elephant responds as the keeper wishes, the elephant receives an apple or other piece of fruit and praise. Over time, and with plenty of patience, the elephants learn the routines.

If, at any time, an elephant does not want to work with the keeper, it simply walks away and the training is over for the day. The keepers never shout or threaten the elephants. Usually, the elephants enjoy the training and the attention they get.

FEET

Training the elephants to present their feet for inspection is very important. Hidden infections can fester in their toenails if their feet are not clean. In the wild, very long walks over rough terrain keep an elephant's feet in good condition. In Dublin Zoo, coarse sand at The Kaziranga Forest Trail and in the elephant houses helps to keep their feet in good condition. However, additional work is required to make sure that the nails and pads of their feet are strong and healthy.

When the keepers want to check their feet, the elephants have been trained to place each foot in a port when requested. The keepers wash their feet, file their nails, check the pads of their feet for problems and clean out any dirt.

Even when they were very young, Asha and Budi were trained to place their feet in a port. Their nails were soft and did not need treatment but the keepers conditioned the young animals to present their feet.

MOVING BUDI

Photo: Budi (below) in a specially designed container

Budi was born in Dublin Zoo in 2008. He had never been constrained or controlled by a human. But when he was moving to Antwerp Zoo, he had to travel in a container. The elephant team spent months preparing him for the move. He was gradually separated from Yasmin, his mother, during training; this allowed them to get used to being apart. A travelling container was specially designed for him and placed in the elephant house for six weeks before he left so he could get used to this too. When he left in July 2012, he was relaxed and went into the container with ease.

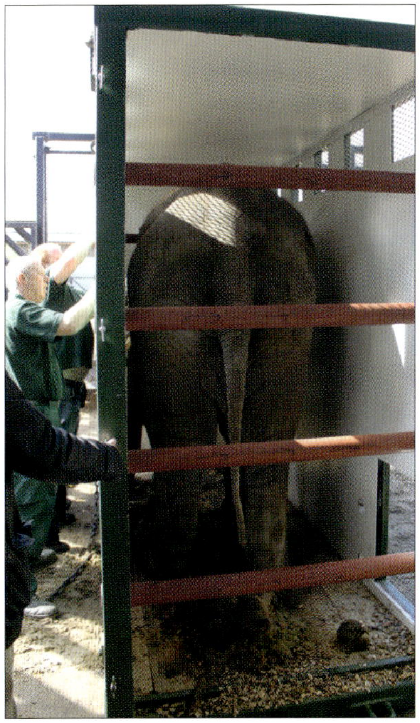

INTERNATIONAL EXPERTISE

Dublin Zoo communicates with international experts and other zoos around the world to develop knowledge and skills in working with elephants. Alan Roocroft, an international expert on elephants, supports the Dublin Zoo team by visiting regularly and giving advice. Jones and Jones Architects and Landscape Architects, the zoo designers in Seattle, helped the Zoo team and the Office of Public Works with the design of The Kaziranga Forest Trail.

Dublin Zoo has an international reputation for the way it looks after its elephants. Zoo professionals come from all over the world to see The Kaziranga Forest Trail and learn from the Dublin Zoo team. Members of the elephant care team are also invited to visit zoos around the world to share their wealth of knowledge.

WITH THANKS TO:

Children of Third Class (2012–13), Queen of the Angels Primary School, Wedgewood, Dublin 16

Molly Coffey-O'Connor

Kate McGowan

James McGowan

Robert Rigby

Richard and Dorothy Vaughton

Mary de Courcy

Maria Rawlins

The entire Dublin Zoo team

Alan Roocroft and The Elephant Management School, Hamburg

The elephant team at Chester Zoo

Dublin Zoo thanks Catherine de Courcy for her research, Cathy Callan for her artwork, Anne Brady and the team at Vermillion for the design of this book.

REFERENCES

British and Irish Association of Zoos and Aquariums: *Elephants: management guidelines for the welfare of zoo animals.* 3rd edition. London, British and Irish Association of Zoos and Aquariums, 2010

Murray E. Fowler and Susan K. Mikota: *Biology, medicine and surgery of elephants.* Ames, Iowa, Blackwell Publications, 2006.

Illustration: Dung Beetle (opposite page)

Dublin Zoo is a registered charity.
Dublin Zoo works in partnership
with zoos worldwide, to make a
significant contribution to the
conservation of the natural
diversity of life on earth.

Published by Associated Editions
33 Melrose Avenue, Dublin 3
on behalf of Dublin Zoo, 2013.
ISBN 978-1-906429-24-9
www.associatededitions.ie

Design by VERMILLON

DUBLIN ZOO

Æ
ASSOCIATED EDITIONS
www.associatededitions.ie